PAMPHLETS ON AMERICAN WRITERS · NUMBER 64

Edna St. Vincent Millay

BY JAMES GRAY

UNIVERSITY OF MINNESOTA PRESS · MINNEAPOLIS

EDNA ST. VINCENT MILLAY

Edna St. Vincent Millay

M ANY years after the death of Edna St. Vincent Millay a friend continued to cherish a memory of the young poet as she had seen her once, flashing up Macdougal Street in Greenwich Village, laughing as she ran, her long hair flying about her shoulders, a young man on her heels earnestly enacting the comedy of pursuit.

The image is pleasing and it is not deceptive as a reflection of the special grace that characterized both the temperament and the literary gift of an artist with a high sense of drama. One recalls inevitably a line by Keats as Edna Millay herself so often did. One sees figures of the classic tradition like many that pervade her own work. There she and her companion are, "forever panting and forever young."

There is the further significance to the recollection that it exactly satisfies the impression left on many of her readers by the poet who presented herself, in an early revelation, as one who was disposed to burn her candle at both ends and to bathe her tantalizingly smiling face in its "lovely light." For the two decades of her ever-rising popularity — the twenties and thirties of the century — she seemed to personify the spirit of the time: its exuberance, its defiance of convention, its determination to discover and to declare a sharply defined identity.

But to remember her only as the nymph of Greenwich Village, exulting playfully in freedom, would be to turn away from nearly all that was of genuine importance to the experience which she put herself to exquisite pain to communicate. Seen whole she emerges out of myth not as a gay figure but as a tragic one; not as

5

a precocious perennial schoolgirl but as an artist born mature and burdened with a scrupulous sense of responsibility toward her gift; not as a changeling child of mysticism but as a creature whose essential desire was to find identity with the balanced order of nature; not as a woman merely but as a creator who inevitably contained within her persona masculine as well as feminine attributes.

The theme of all her poetry is the search for the integrity of the individual spirit. The campaign to conquer and control this realm of experience is conducted always in terms of positive and rigorous conflict — the duel with death, the duel with love, the duel of mind pitted against heart, the duel with "The spiteful and the stingy and the rude," who would steal away possession of beauty.

It is not too fanciful to say that she was born old while she remained forever young, and her personal history explains the fortunate anomaly. Rockland, Maine, was her native place (she was born there on February 22, 1892) and she lived her childhood in a succession of towns in the same state. The parents were separated, and, though Edna Millay communicated freely and amicably with her father, it was to her mother that she gave a devotion earned by the quite extraordinary aptitude for guidance that Cora Millay showed in relationship to her three daughters. Trained to be a singer, the mother took time from her duties as breadwinner, serving as a district nurse, to coach town orchestras and to write out scores for their members. She found time also to teach her daughter Edna to write poetry at the age of four and to play the piano at the age of seven.

Despite the meagerness of the bread-and-butter resources of Cora Millay's matriarchal society its advantages to a buoyant young mentality were many. Opportunities for self-instruction abounded. The daughters contrived theatrical entertainments, produced a body of "instant" folklore, and presented to their world an attrac-

6

tive picture of close-knit solidarity among proto-bohemians exactly of the later Greenwich Village type. Mrs. Millay, removing
a cigarette from her lips to utter mild acerbities at the expense
of mediocre ideals and concessive attitudes, educated her daughters in independence of outlook.

Though she had been awakened early to interests of the arts
and of the mind, Edna Millay had no opportunity to go to college
until she was in her twenties. She was able to receive formal instruction belatedly with the help of a chance acquaintance who,
recognizing unusual quality in a shy girl who had already written
the poem "Renascence," found the money to send her, first, to a
speed-up indoctrination course at Barnard and, then, to Vassar.
She showed herself to be a superior student; acted with spirit, conviction, and talent in many student plays; and, managing to let
love of learning triumph over a distaste for regimentation,
rounded out a highly creditable undergraduate career at twenty-
five. She wrote the baccalaureate hymn for her class and revealed
herself as anything but a schoolgirl versifier by opening it with
these lines:

> Thou great offended God of love and kindness,
>   We have denied, we have forgotten Thee!
> With deafer sense endow, enlighten us with blindness,
>   Who, having ears and eyes, nor hear nor see.

Greenwich Village had become quite recently the febrile state
of mind so well known to social historians, and Edna Millay, immediately upon her arrival in it, became a conspicuous represen-
tative of its temper. Habits of industry combined with inborn discipline enabled her to work simultaneously on three levels of
productivity. She wrote poems which were published in magazines
of prestige as well as in the popular ones of the period. She played
central roles in productions of the Provincetown Players, some
of her own authorship. Under the pseudonym Nancy Boyd she

7

turned out satiric stories and prose sketches which were valued by several editors, among them Frank Crowninshield of *Vanity Fair*. In the Village atmosphere Edna Millay prospered as few American poets had managed up to that time to do. The printed volumes of her poetry went into the hands of an unprecedentedly large following and her popularity was further increased by her appearances in public recitals of her work and by readings over a nationwide hook-up on radio.

As symbolic figure — the "free woman" of the age — Edna Millay could not have eluded close examination of her personal history. This was an interest which the candor of her love poems seemed uninhibitedly to endorse and, as she once made wry confession in a moment of frivolity, she never had "in the presence of clergymen denied these loves." The history of her friendships was intense, filled with *Sturm und Drang*. She seems to have surprised many of her admirers quite out of the usual routine of responses — made up as these often are of inverse vanity and zeal for conquest — into an almost awed awareness of herself as a person, of her glowing particularity. It was perhaps the special grace of her integrity which made her physical attractiveness seem to be even greater in sum than itemized descriptions of eyes, hair, throat, figure added up to. She had gaiety to give but without provocativeness, candor but with no abandonment to license, love in large measure but held within the confines of a somehow austere decorum.

These considerations are relevant to an examination of her work. The same quiet reverence for vitality under discipline is the distinguishing quality of her poetry. At its best it is characterized by a kind of orderly surrender to ecstasy.

She married at last. Eugen Boissevain was an exuberant man of Dutch ancestry who had been a successful man of affairs. He gave up his business as importer when he assumed responsibility for the care of this woman of high talent who became in her early middle years an invalid with physical crises aggravated in crucial instances by what she herself described as "very handsome . . . all but life-size" nervous breakdowns. After two years of marriage filled with gaiety and work the poet and her genial protector retired to a place with which their lives were to be identified for nearly a quarter of a century — Steepletop, near Austerlitz, New York. Their way of life retracted into a simpler pattern partly because of Edna Millay's uncertain health, partly because money difficulties began to press upon them bluntly forbidding bohemian extravagances. But both at the New York farm house and on an island retreat off the coast of Maine friends were received warmly and the severely enforced routine of work was interrupted by the pleasures to which Edna Millay continued to be devoted throughout her days — swimming, bird-watching, gardening, and music-making.

In these settings the poet labored to discipline her gift with the conscientiousness she had always required of herself. But she saw her popularity and her reputation wane. The tragedy of a decline in critical favor was sharpened by the severity of the judgments which she herself made on some of her later products. When she felt that she had written bad poetry she suffered on a level of intensity quite similar to that which she had enjoyed as ecstasy in her happiest and most creative moments.

Eugen Boissevain died suddenly in the fall of 1949 after an operation for a lung condition. A period of haunted loneliness followed for Edna Millay but it lasted only a little more than a year. On a morning in October of 1950 she was found dead on the stairs of Steepletop. Characteristically she had been going to bed with a work of poetry in her hands — the proof pages of Rolfe Humphries' translation of the *Aeneid*.

It is often said of the major figures of the arts that each seems to

9

create a universe all his own and to measure its vast dimensions with untransferable techniques. In the realm of painting this is true of Michelangelo just as, in literature, it is true of Dante and Milton. All three confront us with an overwhelming awareness of Heaven, Earth, and Hell revealed in explicit images and dramatized in a tumult of events. It is true also that Shakespeare created whole societies and civilizations of men and women having such amplitude and luster, such imperious and conflicting passions, that he had to create also a new world to hold them.

No such gigantic stature can be claimed for a poet like Edna Millay. Her theme was too personal, too intimate to herself to fill out the dimensions of a supernatural realm of imagination. Indeed it might be said that her unique effort was to perform the miracle of creation in reverse. A universe already made pressed its weight on the sensibility, the aptitude for awareness, of one individual: "Infinity/Came down and settled over me . . ."

The poet's need is to apprehend the "radiant identity" of life and to embrace it ardently. "World, world, I cannot get thee close enough." This reunion with nature — universal nature — is immediately important to one person, alone and aided only by his own integrity. The search is for the self; the struggle is to be reborn out of chaos to "a sense of glad awakening."

The journey in search of wholeness for the individual, an adventure which has obsessed the minds of the philosophers of the past and the psychiatrists of the present, cannot be left safely to further exploration by the computers of the future. It continues, therefore, to be of no trivial interest as it is presented in the poems of Edna St. Vincent Millay.

It should not be taken as an indication of a failure to grow that Edna Millay produced when she was only nineteen years old one of the most characteristic, most memorable, and most moving of her poems. The intuitions of artists do not reach them on any schedule of merely logical development. All the wisdom they ever attain may be at their command in the beginning. Later statements of it seem to serve chiefly to corroborate or to enrich, out of a diversity of experience that may be tragic without being fatal to faith, the items of the credo as it was first presented. In "Renascence" Edna Millay announced the theme to which four more decades of her life were to be spent in the most intense kind of concentration. "The soul can split the sky in two,/ And let the face of God shine through." This confrontation with the divine can be dared and endured because man is one with the divine.

Edna Millay presented the inner life of the spirit always as a conflict of powerful forces. The will to live and the will to die are elementally at war in "Renascence." Consciousness of the world's misery is so desperately immediate to the poet's imagination that

> For my omniscience paid I toll
> In infinite remorse of soul.
> All sin was of my sinning, all
> Atoning mine, and mine the gall
> Of all regret. . . .

There can be no escape from so formidable a burden of awareness but into the grave. But it is no passive rejection that the spirit experiences. The weight of infinity must be flung off with a gigantic effort.

> And as it went my tortured soul
> Burst forth and fled in such a gust
> That all about me swirled the dust.

The peace of death is achieved and the vulnerable spirit hears from above its hiding place the rain's "friendly sound." The impulse toward surrender *itself* has roused the counter impulse toward a participation more passionate than ever before in the values of human existence. In another convulsion of nature, dra-

11

matizing the imperious contradictions of the spirit, the grave is washed away:

> Ah! Up then from the ground sprang I
> And hailed the earth with such a cry
> As is not heard save from a man
> Who has been dead, and lives again.
> About the trees my arms I wound;
> Like one gone mad I hugged the ground . . .

The meaning of this battle of the wills is clear. The anguish of existence must be endured as the tribute owed to its beauty.

> The world stands out on either side
> No wider than the heart is wide;
> Above the earth is stretched the sky, —
> No higher than the soul is high.

This is the identity between man's nature and the nature of the universe which need only be recognized for the release of incalculable benefits. But an enormous struggle must be waged within the self to establish man's loyalty to the values of life.

An account of the running battle between life and death claimed first place among the poet's preoccupations through her writing career. The effectiveness of the report is heightened by an awareness, sometimes bitter and sometimes merely rueful, that now one side commands ascendancy over will and now the other. In a poem ironically called "Spring" the desperate reproach is offered: "Beauty is not enough." Death is everywhere; with furtive cunning, its forces invade life itself.

But the mood passes. The characteristic one reasserts itself in "The Poet and His Book." Now the plea is for life even after death, the immortality of an imperishable achievement, however small. The poet will live in his book if only the "stranger" can be persuaded to "turn the tattered pages."

Sometimes, as in "Moriturus," the ambivalent attitude begs for an unreasonable indulgence: to have "Two things in one:/ The peace of the grave,/ And the light of the sun . . ." But the fantastic notion of a reconciliation between life and death fades in a moment. Militant life asserts its claims more positively than ever before. Death is stripped of the majesty in which fear has slavishly dressed him. He is discovered to be nothing: "He is less/ Than Echo answering/ 'Nothingness!' " The will to live mounts through many crisp and angry stanzas. The poet allows raillery to creep into her declaration of war. She speaks like a housewife who has quite enough of irrelevant harassments as she declares that she will hold death off by "bolting" her door "with a bolt and a cable;/ I shall block my door/ With a bureau and a table . . ." But she means every savage and decisive word as death is finally warned that

> With his hand on my mouth
> He shall drag me forth,
> Shrieking to the south
> And clutching at the north.

It is indicative of a striking consistency of outlook even in the midst of the poet's conflicts that in this prophetic vision of what her doomed battle with death will be she reaffirms vigorously her sense of identity with the universe. The world is still no wider than the heart is wide. She shrieks for help to the south as if it were her close ally and clutches at the north, feeling it to be a possession that is being unjustly torn from her.

As she grew older the tone of her quarrel with death tended to become more subdued. In "Dirge without Music" the inevitability of the loss of the valued people of her life is grudgingly accepted. But the wasteful pattern of existence is nonetheless rebuked with a kind of womanly primness:

> Down, down, down into the darkness of the grave
> Gently they go, the beautiful, the tender, the kind;

> Quietly they go, the intelligent, the witty, the brave.
> I know. But I do not approve. And I am not resigned.

This understatement is more moving than a harangue by a bitter fatalist could be. Tucked neatly away into the reticence of the judgment is the suggestion that, as one who is closely identified with nature, the poet could have managed things better if her human insight had been allowed to prevail. Such variations of tone in her report on the duel of life against death lend the best and most original of her personal qualities to the development of an old, familiar theme. The parallel may be suggested that, just as a mother must have faith in her child lacking any evidence to justify it, so the believer in life must show a similar courageous unreasonableness. Edna Millay is perhaps at her best when she casts her vote of No Confidence in death.

During the 1930's and the 1940's history with its stubborn, mindless reiteration of the chants of war deposited its grievous weight on Edna Millay's imagination. Inevitably the theme of life against death found its most tragic variation as she seized bitterly on the drama of life becoming actually the ally of death. She endured the sufferings of the time not merely as any sensitive noncombatant must but rather as one who, having been conscious always of the crucial character of the conflict between creative and destructive forces, felt deeply involved in what might well prove to be a final defeat for humankind.

But in the poems of this period her protest against death is put forward no less vigorously than before simply because the ecstasy of rebirth has become far less easy to evoke. In "Apostrophe to Man (on reflecting that the world is ready to go to war again)" a formidable denunciation is hurled at the world's whole company of men and women: "Detestable race, continue to expunge yourself, die out./ Breed faster, crowd, encroach, sing hymns, build bombing airplanes . . ." Indignation at the will to die bursts out not merely from the scattered pronouncements of such staccato verse; it is present also in the most elegantly polished of the sonnets, mixing pity with despair in equally bitter parts. The sequence to which she gives the over-all title "Epitaph for the Race of Man" presents her misgiving at its most bleak. A vision is summoned up of the planet about to grow cold after the final suicide of humankind. "Man and his engines be no longer here."

> High on his naked rock the mountain sheep
> Will stand alone against the final sky,
> Drinking a wind of danger new and deep,
> Staring on Vega with a piercing eye,
> And gather up his slender hooves and leap
> From crag to crag down Chaos, and so go by.

But the militant mind is not truly ready even now for any such tight-lipped acceptance. The belief in rebirth is too powerful to crumple under the worst of threats. New visions and new hopes break through. The poet sees man waking in terror in the night to find the almost but not quite final disaster hurtling down upon his house: "a pitchy lake of scalding stone." Suddenly her faith in his cunning and his resolution is roused again.

> Where did he weep? Where did he sit him down
> And sorrow, with his head between his knees?
> Where said the Race of Man, "Here let me drown"?
> "Here let me die of hunger"? — "let me freeze"?
> By nightfall he has built another town:
> This boiling pot, this clearing in the trees.

So, engulfed in global madness, the poet's belief in the will to live cannot be driven from an unyielding intelligence. She has indeed rejected the witty young woman's notion that "a bureau and a table" will be enough to bar the intrusion of defeatist sentiment. She might be addressing the early, overconfident self when she suggests that a maturity born of experience is needed to "broaden the sensitive/ Fastidious pale perception . . ." No emotion, however inevitable or however blameless, may assume control over the regenerative will. "I must not die of pity; I must live." Nor is it enough simply to stay alive; ecstasy must be reclaimed. The poet will "pour away despair/ And rinse the cup, eat happiness like bread."

Triumphantly something quite like the tone of "Renascence" declares itself anew.

> Thou famished grave, I will not fill thee yet,
> Roar though thou dost, I am too happy here;
> Gnaw thine own sides, fast on; I have no fear
> Of thy dark project, but my heart is set
> On living — I have heroes to beget
> Before I die . . .

So many of Edna Millay's pages are devoted to critical moments of the love duel that it has been possible, even for reasonably well informed readers, to be aware only of her confidences about "what arms have lain/ Under my head till morning." To their loss they have ignored her equal preoccupation with other themes. Still it is true that some of her most searching observations about the human condition are concerned with the approach to ecstasy through the identification of man with woman. It would, however, be to deceive oneself to approach these poems as if they were exercises in eroticism. Despite the many sidelong references to the physical relationship, the enclosing interest is that of human love as a total experience of the psyche involving, on the positive side, intellectual communication and sympathy of taste and, on the negative side, the endless warfare of two egos that cannot effect a complete surrender into oneness.

The limp endorsement of correct and appropriate sentiments which has made up so much of love poetry, particularly that written by women, is conspicuous for its total absence from these ardent but anxious confrontations of man and woman. It is significant of Edna Millay's approach to the psychological crisis of love versus hate — and to the even more destructive tragicomedy of love slackening away into indifference by the influences of time, change, and disillusion — that she does not speak of these matters simply as a woman. Often in her highly dramatic representations of the love duel she assumes the man's role and she plays it with no nervous air of indulging in a masquerade. She is concerned with the mind as the retort in which all the chemical reactions of love take place and, because her own intelligence partook of both masculine and feminine characteristics, the poems convey the impression that the exactitude of science, in control of the impulses of intuition, has been brought to bear to reveal much that those changes involve in a man's temperament as well as in a woman's.

Again, as in her account of the conflict of the will to live and the will to die, the love duel is presented with high drama as one that is destined to go on and on indecisively because the adversaries are only too well matched in aggressiveness and submissiveness, in strength and weakness, in sympathy and treachery.

The ecstatic instant, captured with a delicate but firm precision in many of the love poems, found what is perhaps its best expression in Sonnet I of *Fatal Interview*. The sight of human love is set before us through the eyes of a god. Hermes, airborne by his winged sandals, skims over "a pearled and roseate plain beneath." Then, unintelligibly at first, he feels the intervention between himself and his goal of a force from earth. The immeasurable distance between divine sense and human sense obscures the meaning of the encounter, but at last the god becomes aware of a concentration of passion more intimate, more pure, than any a god has ever known. His response is one of rueful jealousy. He asks himself how it can be that man, the creature "built of salt and lime" whose "borrowed breath" must presently send him "labouring to a doom I may not feel," has found, nonetheless, an incomparable blessing to allevi-

ate, even to justify, the pain of his journey to a "dusty end."
Hermes feels "the proud eyes of bliss" turned upon him. He is
almost tempted to reject his divine condition that he may identify
himself with creatures so to be envied. "Up, up, my feathers! — ere
I lay you by/ To journey barefoot with a mortal joy."

The reverential gaiety of this mood, which finds room for humor
in the midst of the contemplation of bliss, characterizes much of
Edna Millay's love poetry. Its popularity may be accounted for by
the intoxicating quality that brings the immediacy of a highly personal emotion to the poetic statement. The merit that gives the
work permanence is the fastidiousness of the style in which the
spontaneity is captured.

In her younger days Edna Millay sometimes allowed her exuberant vitality to escape into verses the levity of which made her
famous, perhaps to the injury of her reputation as a serious poet.
There are, for example, the eminently quotable lines of "Thurs-
day."

> And if I loved you Wednesday,
>   Well, what is that to you?
> I do not love you Thursday —
>   So much is true.
>
> And why you come complaining
>   Is more than I can see.
> I loved you Wednesday, — yes — but what
>   Is that to me?

These flourishes of audacity do not touch at all closely on the
center of her understanding of the love duel. There she held a
formidable awareness of the power of change which is not in the
least like the vague consciousness of impermanence in which so
many poetic spirits have fluttered with languid futility. Swin-
burne "sighs" that "no love endures." The fact that it was a badly
tarnished stereotype of emotion when he uttered it has not dis-

suaded romantics from echoing it ever since. Edna Millay used the sharpest tools of her intelligence to hew out for herself a unique place among poets by undertaking to discover *why* no love endures. What she says is that the loophole in commitment offers the necessary escape route by which the self saves its integrity. There can be no such thing as total surrender except with degradation or with, what is worse, dishonesty. In love the giving must be generous and free, but there must be withholding, too, if the self is to remain whole. In Sonnet XLVII of *Fatal Interview* the point is made:

> Well, I have lost you; and I lost you fairly
> In my own way, and with my full consent.
> If I had loved you less or played you slyly
> I might have held you for a summer more,
> But at the cost of words I value highly . . .

It is understood in advance that the reward of this conscientiousness will be to know the full bitterness of the loss, for "Time does not bring relief; you all have lied/ Who told me Time would ease me of my pain."

The immediacy of experience is communicated in images that are piercingly personal. Very often the suggestions of the figurative language are so unexpected that they seem to spring out of an immediate passion which catches deliberately and desperately at punishing words. Love has been "stung to death by gnats." "My kisses now are sand against your mouth,/ Teeth in your palm and pennies on your eyes." Only out of the whirlwind of an unstudied grief could a voice speak with just this accent.

It is because she was bold enough to examine the problem of the psychological distance between man and woman — one that cannot be breached and should not be violated — that Edna Millay may be said to have made an original contribution to the literature of the love duel.

In the sonnet called "Bluebeard" she assumes the voice of a man speaking to an importunate woman.

> This door you might not open, and you did;
> So enter now, and see for what slight thing
> You are betrayed. . . . Here is no treasure hid . . .

Yet the private consciousness is valuable, even in its meagerness, precisely because it is private.

> Look yet again:
> An empty room, cobwebbed and comfortless.
> Yet this alone out of my life I kept
> Unto myself, lest any know me quite . . .

To violate this sanctuary is to destroy love.

> And you did so profane me when you crept
> Unto the threshold of this room tonight
> That I must never more behold your face.
> This now is yours. I seek another place.

The tragedy of rejection has its counterpart in the tragedy of acceptance. The poem called "On the Wide Heath" in effect tells the Bluebeard story again with the temper of the actor presented exactly in reverse. Against a bleak background a man on foot makes his way toward home at nightfall. He knows what sort of scene awaits him. He will enter there "The kitchen of a loud shrew" to find besides his wife "a wordless poaching son and a daughter/ With a disdainful smile . . ." Then with the deftness and economy of means that she had learned in the theater the poet springs her appalling surprise. The man is willing to go

> Home to the worn reproach, the disagreeing
> The shelter, the stale air; content to be
> Pecked at, confined, encroached upon, — it being
> Too lonely, to be free.

Again it is the ability to capture in colloquial language and in one brief thunderclap of drama the essence of a tragic psychological struggle that lends to Edna Millay's long discussion of the love duel its effects of variety and flexibility.

The tone of melancholy misgiving in the face of the emotional crisis is pervasive in these studies. But the warming, the nourishing, the half-maternal aspects of the experience of love are not neglected. In Sonnet LI of *Fatal Interview* Edna Millay echoes a sentiment to which Shakespeare gave a masculine accent. Her feminine version seems no less eloquent, no less moving:

> If in the years to come you should recall
> When faint at heart or fallen on hungry days,
> Or full of griefs and little if at all
> From them distracted by delights or praise;
> When failing powers or good opinion lost
> Have bowed your neck, should you recall to mind
> How of all men I honoured you the most,
> Holding you noblest among mortal-kind:
> Might not my love — although the curving blade
> From whose wide mowing none may hope to hide,
> Me long ago below the frosts had laid —
> Restore you somewhat to your former pride?
> Indeed I think this memory, even then,
> Must raise you high among the run of men.

It is characteristic of Edna Millay's temper — not merely its prevailing but its almost uninterrupted mood — that she enters upon the search for beauty as if this, too, were a struggle. In the poem called "Assault" she blurts out the half-welcoming, half-fearful exclamation: "I am waylaid by Beauty." There is no coyness in this air of alarm. To the acutely alerted sensibilities of eyes and ears beauty reveals many aspects and sounds in different voices. She hears it in the croaking of a frog quite as clearly as in the song of a skylark, and each declaration of its presence is something to be appraised with scrupulous attention. She speaks sometimes of "savage beauty." Even when the impact on her senses is not violent it is still an experience to be received warily — on guard. Beauty in the guise of April is challenged with the suggestion that it comes with crafty intent like a seducer. "You can no longer quiet me with the redness/ Of little leaves opening stickily./ I know what I know."

This is to say that the mind has its right to evaluate beauty. It should not yield in limp acceptance as if faced by something of divine origin and therefore, like a god of Greek mythology, not to be denied its will. What Edna Millay persuades a reader that she does indeed know is that beauty must be endured as well as enjoyed. To surrender to beauty without resistance would be to lose an exhilarating aspect of the experience. It must be participated in, but the terms of one's compact with beauty must be understood to be one-sided. "Beauty makes no pledges." In return for the awe that the observer feels in its presence nothing is promised other than awareness itself. Beauty manifests itself in the glow of a bird's wing and in the rotting limb of a tree; it exists in monumental forms and in minute ones. But in the ardent search for its benefits, great or small, the disciple must never forget that his devotion must be to an influence that continues serenely to be godlike, aloof, and impersonal. "Beauty never slumbers/ All is in her name."

That she is not entirely consistent in developing her religion of beauty need not be found disturbing. She is no more given to shifts of interpretation than mystics must ever be. Beauty may be aloof and impersonal but it is also an element in the process of rebirth, the faith in which the poet takes her deepest comfort. It even becomes in certain poems the food on which she feeds. Her figures of speech suggest again and again that, as a woman, she felt an almost organic closeness to the working of gestation. A conscientious expectant mother, she will search for beauty even "where beauty never stood . . ./ Having a growing heart to feed."

Part of the nourishment that she receives from awareness of beauty is provided by what is for her the immediate actuality of sensuous experience. Better than any imagining is the presence in the eye of a satisfying scene or the reverberation in the ear of lovely sound.

> Not, to me, less lavish — though my dreams have been
> splendid —
> Than dreams, have been the hours of the actual day:
> Never, awaking, did I awake to say:
> "Nothing could be like that," when a dream was ended.
> Colours, in dream; ecstasy, in dream extended
> Beyond the edge of sleep — these, in their way,
> Approach, come even closer, yet pause, yet stay . . .

The experiences of the actual, which she goes on to enumerate as containers of ecstasy, include those offered by "Music, and painting, poetry, love, and grief." Then at the close of the sonnet her pantheistic faith in the oneness and the continuity of nature reasserts itself. Real and reassuring to her are the harmony of opposites, the unity that may be resolved out of contradictions, and the inevitability of rebirth following decay. Beauty can be endured because the poet has been able to convince herself in the end that "the budding and the falling leaf" are "one, and wonderful, — not to be torn / Apart."

In "Moriturus" the young artist warned the world with humorous defiance that she would "take it hard" when death threatened her. It was precisely because she continued throughout her life to take it hard, when she was confronted by confusing manifestations of beauty, that she was able to communicate so great a sense of vitality to each phase of the adventure. She was always an actor in the drama: a militant defender of herself against beauty, a militant defender of beauty against its defilers. And she was resolutely faithful to the integrity of her own perceptions. She never attempts to encompass more of a sense of the wonder of the natural world than her own eyes can see. What moves her is the recollection of a familiar scene, fixed in memory by some small detail of local color. Significance is imparted to the image by a subtle infusion of the poet's emotion as she remembers this glimpse of the seacoast or that corner of a city street: "Eager vines/ Go up the rocks and wait"; "These wet rocks where the tide has been,/ Barnacled white and weeded brown"; "Yellow leaves along the gutters/ In the blue and bitter fall." Armed with awareness, the one who is "waylaid" by beauty may find exultation in the simplest of experiences. Edna Millay did indeed seem to write all her poems to give permanence to a moment of ecstasy.

It was not merely in encounters with nature that she felt herself to be encompassed by beauty and deeply involved in a struggle to receive its blessing. She wrestled with the angel in the realm of art and also in that of pure intellectual effort. Two of the most memorable of her sonnets dramatize these vigorous exercises of the spirit.

The words "On Hearing a Symphony of Beethoven" may suggest that the poet has, for once, been reduced to a mood of passive receptivity, willing to receive beauty ready-made and placative. But that was never Edna Millay's temper. Even as listener she was participant in a struggle to earn the benefit of an experience. In this poem she seizes upon music as another instrument for finding out the truth that is implicit in beauty. Not too much — though something — may be made of the fact that Edna Millay, her mother's daughter, knew many musical scores in as much detail as does even the most conscientious of orchestra conductors. But it was not from the circumstances of being well instructed that her responsiveness sprang. In her seat at a concert she was able to become a collaborator in the creative undertaking because creativity was ever the spontaneous impulse of mind and senses working together.

So, in the sonnet, Beethoven's achievement becomes hers by right of possession. She does not hold that right with vague gratification. She grapples with it, prepared to do battle for it. "Sweet sounds, oh, beautiful music do not cease!/ Reject me not into the world again." The meaning of what she hears is something broader and deeper than any discipline in the technique of musical composition could make intelligible. Here again is the message of rebirth, another statement of the inextinguishable virtue of vigorous creative effort. The truth implicit in this beauty is vital and vivifying. "Mankind made plausible, his purpose plain." The poet's supercharged awareness drives several ways at once toward comprehension. A pantheistic vision of the oneness of all life — suffering, decaying yet surviving — suggests the line "The tranquil blossom on the tortured stem." Tranquillity and torture: they, also, are "one, and wonderful, — not to be torn/Apart." Not in nature, not in the music of Beethoven, not in the responsive intelligence of Edna St. Vincent Millay.

It is of inescapable significance that in a poem which on the surface seems merely to explore the most pallid of academic interests, "music appreciation," there should be so many words which describe a militant stance, an attitude of defensive wariness in the face of an adversary: "Reject me not," "scatter [my towers]," "my rampart." If the sonnet seems to have an untarnished originality of temper, after many years of familiarity with it, that must be because Edna Millay dares to suggest that the enemies of "man's purpose" are not merely the formidable ones who scatter destruction in the form of bombs. There are other enemies whom she identifies as "The spiteful and the stingy and the rude," who devastate the landscape of the spirit with showers of tawdry and mediocre values. In defense of the purposes of life it is necessary to be ready to do battle on all fronts against not merely the great incalculable forces of "Doom," which must inevitably espy our towers in the end, but also against those who undermine our ramparts with the erosive agents of meanness and vulgarity.

The other sonnet describes an even more original adventure in search of beauty. A surprising and highly specialized sort of sensibility is involved in this exercise. Edna Millay was in fact a highly skilled amateur in the science of mathematics and she might well have just put away some self-assigned task in the field when she wrote "Euclid Alone Has Looked on Beauty Bare." But it is not really a celebration of the aesthetics of geometry that is contained in this poem. The enclosing mood is that of reverence for the intelligence of man. This creature, whom she has often described as deserving only pity for his weakness or scorn for his perversity, is capable, in moments when his essential genius has just been born anew, of seizing upon knowledge in a dazzling flash of lucidity. With little to guide him but his self-instructed technique of divination he dares to explore the very depths of abstract thought: "O blinding hour, O holy, terrible day,/ When first the shaft into his vision shone/ Of light anatomized!" The unique drama of this foray into a realm of learning — one that not merely was uncharted but had not previously even been imagined to exist — needs no underscoring. In her deft summation of the significance of the experience, as its effects ray out and touch all men everywhere, Edna Millay contents herself with one personal comment:

> Euclid alone
> Has looked on Beauty bare. Fortunate they
> Who, though once only and then but far away,
> Have heard her massive sandal set on stone.

Sober gratitude for the privilege of perceiving beauty has, in this sonnet, its most characteristic expression. But there is another implication to be read between the lines touching on the central theme of the poet's long debate with man. What is tragic for her is the irony that a being with the audacity to claim for himself such awesome attributes of mind should often allow his nature to be degraded by negative attributes of pettiness. She is appalled to see his grandeur dissipated — as she might have said, using words that she applied to the loss of love — "in little ways."

From first to last, through every phase of her development, Edna Millay continued to be intensely herself and no other. Whether her theme was death, love, beauty, or the refreshing impulse of the will to live she spoke always with an accent that was unique to her. Of language she made a homespun garment to clothe her passions and her faith.

That she was able to create effects of striking originality is discovered to be only the more remarkable when a characteristic poem is examined closely and its thought is found to wear "something old" and "something borrowed" from the left-over wardrobe of tradition. Edna Millay was a product as much of the nineteenth century as of the twentieth. The influence of tradition moved her a little backward in time. A too great reverence for her early instruction — not only at her mother's knee but also at Keats's — probably accounts for all the "O's" and "Ah's," the "would I were's," the "hast's," the "art's," the "wert's," the " 'Tis's." It must account also for the inversions of normal word order which sometimes impede the plunge of her hardihood in thought.

Even in more important matters of vocabulary, imagery, and symbolism her impulse toward expression was governed by convention. Despite her interest in science she felt its discipline to be alien to her always personal style of utterance. She did not find in its language a new source of imaginative power such as Auden has exploited. Despite her obsession in the late years with the crisis of war, such a reference as one to "Man and his engines" reveals an uninvolved attitude toward the special concerns of the machine age. The hoe, as symbol, was an instrument of which she was intensely hand-conscious but the airplane's power seemed not to have for her the figurative significance that it had for Randall Jarrell. Despite the fact that she grew up in the shadow of Freud and must have participated in endless talk about the ego and the id in the loft-studios of Greenwich Village, she was not prompted to follow the leads of psychology and psychiatry down into the caves of memory as were Jeffers and Warren. The familiar image, drawn from the treasury of metaphor upon which Shakespeare also depended for imaginative resource, seems never to have dismayed her. She was not inhibited by fear of intelligibility; she was not tempted to prod the imagination with tortured similes. For her, death still swung his scythe and the poems in which he does so with the old familiar ruthlessness betray no nervous apprehension that the instrument may have become rusty or blunted with the use of ages.

Because she absorbed tradition deeply into herself she seems able to revitalize its language with the warmth of her own temper. Her words become fertile from the nourishment which, as woman, she communicated to them as if by an umbilical link.

Simplicity, spontaneity, the seeming absence of calculation combine to produce her best effects. An apron that has fallen from a clothesline and lain all winter in a snow drift until it has become stiff with frost may still be restored, soft and pliable, to appropriate purposes of housewifely solicitude and care. This, as a symbol of restoration, is one that could have come into the mind only of an observer who trusted her own intuitions. Associations of idea between enormous plight and commonplace remedy never fail to stimulate this alert and resourceful imagination. Edna Millay blocks death's way "with a bureau and a table," convinced of her own rightness in seizing upon this urgent, though rudimentary, tactic of defense. If the overtone of humor is lost upon the literal ear that matters comparatively little. What she conveys with a surprising freshness is the thought that, in the enormously important struggle to survive, any immediate and awful crisis must be faced with the means ready to hand.

Often she speaks in the voice of a woman engaged in a familiar chore of the common round. But the task becomes symbolic of the urgent need to keep the forces of life alive in threatening circumstances. A housewife lighting a fire on her hearth must ". . . thrust her breath against the stubborn coal,/ Bringing to bear upon its hilt the whole/ Of her still body."

Sometimes the accent of a man is heard as he considers the ultimate defeat of all his hopes, as tiller of the land, under the encompassing blight of war. The blessing of rebirth has been cancelled and he sees the vast emergency shrunk, in all the irreversible trend of devastation, to the dimensions of one of his own fields. Once more the graphic representation is small but complete.

> No toil
> Of rake or hoe, no lime, no phosphate, no rotation
> of crops, no irrigation of the land,
> Will coax the limp and flattened grain to stand
> On that bad day . . .

More often than with either definitely declared voice she speaks as a detached observer of natural sights and sounds. These souvenirs of experience are shared with a reader in language that seems entirely casual; it has been borrowed for the moment from more studied performers in the realm of poetry simply to convey a passing impression. A stream separated into two parts by stones attracts a wanderer's attention. An impression of "The soft, antiphonal speech of the doubled brook" must be recorded simply because it is something charming to remember. More typical of the poet's method is the device of catching a symbolic significance, some warning of the threat against survival, in an image that seems to be, all at once, spontaneous, startling, and inescapably true.

"The Buck in the Snow" brings together the assets of surprising imagery, symbolic overtone, and touching comment. The observer has watched the deer and his mate in the orchard on a winter day.

> I saw them suddenly go,
> Tails up, with long leaps lovely and slow,
> Over the stone-wall into the wood of hemlocks
> bowed with snow.

Later she comes on the buck, shot and left to die. "Now lies he here, his wild blood scalding the snow." Life and death, together; heat and cold, inseparable. And the observer imagines the plight of the mate.

> a mile away by now, it may be,
> Under the heavy hemlocks that as the moments pass
> Shift their loads a little, letting fall a feather
> of snow —
> Life, looking out attentive through the eyes of the doe.

In no poem is there a better example of Edna Millay's gift for blending the archaic with the colloquial than in the "Ballad of the Harp-Weaver." The literary form is borrowed from the past and its sentiment, which plays with unapologetic tenderness on the theme of maternal love, seems somehow antique in a day, such as these of the 1960's, when the ballad has regained wide favor but is used chiefly as mouthpiece for social protest. In Edna Millay's poem a kind of utilitarian fantasy such as only she could have imagined suggests to a poverty-stricken woman that she can weave from the strings of her harp "the clothes of a king's son." The treatment of this delicate material is successful because the poet uses only the commonplaces of everyday speech to evoke a mood of touching benevolence. In the Monday morning language, associated with the simplest kind of domesticity, she persuades even the least pliable reader to be glad that fragile whim has transcended reality. For example, the mother addresses her child:

"Little skinny shoulder-blades
    Sticking through your clothes!
And where you'll get a jacket from
    God above knows.

"It's lucky for me, lad,
    Your daddy's in the ground
And can't see the way I let
    His son go around!"

It is not unlikely that in this experiment — the exact like of which she never again attempted — Edna Millay paid tribute to her mother. To a sensitive and loyal daughter it must have seemed to be almost literally a fact that Cora Millay wove out of music a warm security for her children. What is of chief interest, however, is that in this instance Edna Millay herself wove out of a combination of literary tradition, family tradition, sentiment, and memory an experience as simple and universal as any to be found in the extensive literature of balladry.

An important element in the highly personal tone of all her poetry is the wit that flashes through not merely the exercises in light vein but her most serious reflections as well. The epigram was for her an entirely spontaneous form of expression and its un-expected sparkle of insight often illuminates even the darkest moments of the sonnets.

In the early poems wit is used often with deliberately audacious intent. It mocks at prudery, at self-deception, at all the false senti-ments of the *unco guid*. Typical is the much-quoted poem about the "little Sorrow/ Born of a little Sin." The nymph of Greenwich Village trying to be penitent finds "a room all damp with gloom/ And shut us all within." The tone of raillery foretells the end. The "little Sorrow would not weep," the "little Sin would go to sleep."

So up I got in anger,
    And took a book I had,

> And put a ribbon on my hair
> To please a passing lad,
> And, "One thing there's no getting by —
> I've been a wicked girl," said I;
> "But if I can't be sorry, why,
> I might as well be glad!"

From the standpoint of a sympathetic reader another thing "there's no getting by" is that this poem has serious flaws. The second line of the last stanza is clumsily thrust in to occupy space and to provide a rhyme. The third and fourth owe more to the tradition of Housman (and his small standing army of "light-foot lads") than Edna Millay who wished only to cultivate her own voice should have been willing to pay. But the epigram of the final two lines justifies the effort. Seldom has virtue, in lugubrious false face, been dismissed from the scene with such enviable and persuasive high spirit.

Edna Millay's wit was never petty. She was generous toward all her adversaries except mediocrity, war, and death. And in fashioning an epigram she revealed her most fastidious respect both for truth and for elegance. In the later poems her wit is so unobtrusive, so modest, that it might be missed entirely by a reader hoping to find a showy attribute identified by a capital letter. But it is always subtly present, embedded in a theme, as is the wit of Henry James. The tight-packed phrase, the unexpected revelation of how opposites of impulse may be found to blend, the sudden illumination of an ambiguity — these are the veins of wisdom through which wit runs in the sonnets. In the one numbered xl in *Collected Sonnets* the subject is once more the love duel. Here a struggle is enacted between heart and mind, between imprecisely defined loyalties and the subtly destructive impulses of treachery. Fiction and drama have often dealt at length with such crises; Edna Millay compresses the conflict between loving-obsessively and still-not-loving-enough into fourteen lines. The epigrammatic couplet at the end reveals the subtle quality of the dilemma. A woman reminds herself that she will continue to consume her life in preoccupation with one face "Till all the world, and I, and surely you,/ Will know I love you, whether or not I do."

Edna Millay's wit is not always bittersweet. It can be galling and acidulous. In the sonnet "To Jesus on His Birthday," the poet rejects hypocrisy once more, this time with uncompromising severity. She is appalled, as she sits at a Christmas service, by the magisterial cynicism with which a "humble gospel" is betrayed to please "the proud." Her anger is too great to be disciplined and she snatches hastily for words into the vocabulary of scorn. "Up goes the man of God before the crowd;/ With voice of honey and with eyes of steel . . ." But the shopworn metaphors — voice of honey, eyes of steel — betray only a momentary loss of control. Speaking once more in her own unaffected voice the poet utters an epigram of devastating effectiveness: "The stone the angel rolled away with tears/ Is back upon your mouth these thousand years."

A close examination of the work of any artist is certain to reveal flaws. The very urgency of the desire to communicate must tempt any poet sometimes to override obstacles recklessly. With Edna Millay the individual line seldom limps though it may now and again betray an obvious determination to be vigorous. There is little sense of strain in the use of rhyme and, even in the early poems when her effects threaten to become self-conscious, she avoids the temptation to indulge in the verbal acrobatics of clever versifiers as even Byron does. What troubles her appraisers most of all is the willingness to snatch up old trophies of metaphor and set them up among her own inspirations as if she were unaware of the difference of freshness between them.

But in the end vigor and spontaneity prevail in technique as they do in passion. The singing quality of the lyrics, of the free forms of verse and of the formal sonnets, too, is consistently clear and true. A reader gratefully accepts — as she herself does — the intoxicating stimulation of the air she breathes.

Throughout her life Edna Millay's chief concern was to canalize creative energy into the production of poems that bespoke her innermost awarenesses. In her last years this concentration became so intense that almost all other interests were severely excluded. Yet in earlier phases she was responsive to challenges of many kinds. The world which she felt to be "No wider than the heart is wide" pressed in upon her and made various demands of that heart. Never the sort of artist whose blood becomes frozen in the veins at the touch of an outside influence, she showed herself to be flexible, adaptable, and — sometimes to her disadvantage — willing to take on the coloration of political, social, and moral crises of immediate moments.

She wrote prose, as she wrote poetry, with an at once witty and intensely sober regard for her own values. The personal letters glow — sometimes they seem feverishly to glitter — with the élan that sustained her, however precariously, through the crucial moments of her experience. Her preface to the volume of Baudelaire translations reveals a critical intelligence of distinction. Only the adroit satiric sketches written under the pseudonym Nancy Boyd depart from her preoccupation with poetry. These exercises, too, display a kind of coloratura virtuosity. They draw freely on her gift of wit and have importance as lucid indirect reflections of her attitudes: her unwavering honesty, her distaste for pretense, sentimentality, and concessiveness.

More sympathetic to her essential interests were her experiments in the theater prompted, at first, by loyalty to the innovative purposes of the Provincetown Players. These and later productions for other sponsors all took the form of poetry. As actress *manquée*, Edna Millay understood the various involvements of the drama and faced the most difficult problems that it has to offer with characteristic conscientiousness and flexibility.

Aria da Capo is her most successful expression in dramatic form. This statement of her indignation at man's will to die is stripped down to the essentials of parable; its power is that of a surprise attack on the sensibilities. Using the figures of the traditional theater — Pierrot, Columbine, and a group of shepherds — she puts into the mouths of these unalarming folk colloquial utterances which reveal the tragedy of her conviction that war — always and everywhere — flares ironically out of a blend of lethargy and meanness.

Two young men tending their flocks relieve their boredom by playing at the game of building a wall between their fields. It is woven out of colored crepe paper and becomes a symbol as solidly effective for theatrical purposes as the material and the human motive involved are flimsy. Immediately the existence of a divisive influence creates hostility. In a succession of minute episodes jealousy develops out of whim and baseness out of jealousy until, in the end, the two contrive to kill each other. In the rehearsal for a play which encloses the parable, Pierrot and Columbine represent the society which, with slack disregard for human good, frivolously ignores the disaster. The man bespeaks the mind turned cynical by awareness of evil; the girl, mere mindlessness. Pierrot says: ". . . You see, I am always wanting/ A little more than what I have — or else/ A little less . . ." In the simple complexity of the treatment these themes are allowed to declare their momentous significance. The drama is directly on target and its very brevity increases the effectiveness of impact.

A late experiment with verse drama, *Conversation at Midnight*, reached the stage almost a quarter of a century after it was published and more than a decade after the poet's death. In effect the author of "The Poet and His Book" echoed the early plea "Do not let me die." The tenacious intelligence showed its familiar variability and vitality in a New York production which found faithful adherents. Another performance by a Los Angeles group gave the work not merely a *succès d'estime* but an extended run.

Yet *Conversation at Midnight* remains pseudo-drama, lacking a concentrated drive toward effective vicarious experience. Edna Millay herself considered it to be "an interesting book" but "not really a play." The original manuscript, lost in a fire, had to be reproduced out of memory after the first creative urgency had lost its force. The result is, as she wrote, "jerky and patchy," an often awkward parade of attitudes forced into the form of stage dialogue but lacking the genuine fervor of conflict.

The faults of the work are inherent in the original concept. This requires a group of men, met for a session of late-night drinking and ratiocination, to use the occasion for a kind of war game in which they fire rounds of ammunition over each other's heads, hitting only distant, theoretical targets. Each guest represents a point of view, aesthetic, social, or moral; each in turn has his say, in a piece of stylized elocution, about capitalism, Communism, commercialism, Nazism, and, of course, love in a world that is out of sorts with spontaneity. All is spoken in earnest; much of the talk is witty and stimulating; some of it inevitably seems trivial in its cloudy references to situations in the lives of the characters which there has been neither time nor occasion really to evoke. Nothing resembling dramatic tension can rise out of these arguments which never intermingle, never affect each other, never in the end manage to clarify idea.

A different kind of problem is presented by *The King's Henchman*. Commissioned by the Metropolitan Opera Association of New York to provide a libretto for a score by Deems Taylor, Edna

Millay worked with her usual intensity of conscientiousness to serve the tradition of music to which she was devoted. Her narrative, drawn from sources of legend similar to those which have prompted the many retellings of the Tristram and Isolde story, found dedicated admirers among those who heard the dozen and more performances of the opera given at the Metropolitan itself or the performances of the traveling company which presented it to a wide American audience. The austere dignity of *The King's Henchman*, it must be observed, rebukes for their banal and vulgar triviality the passions of many of the most conspicuous figures of operatic tradition, including those of *Madame Butterfly, La Traviata,* and *The Girl of the Golden West.* The experiment added a significant page to the history of opera in America.

And yet the technique of music drama remained foreign to Edna Millay's direct, candid, personal style of communication. The conventions of the medium dimmed with artificial grandeur the flashes of intuition which illuminate her more characteristic considerations of the love duel. She herself made uncompromisingly severe judgment upon the work. In a letter to her publisher, reconsidering her work in the theater, she tells of trying to rework a spoken drama out of *The King's Henchman.* But the result, she wrote, was "hopelessly contaminated. It smells of libretto." This she thought a pity because, as she went on to say, "some of my very best poetry is to be found in *The King's Henchman, —* to be found, that is, by a reader tough enough to struggle through acres of ostentatious and pedantic drivel in order to get to it."

Under a blast of criticism so withering an impersonal appraiser of the work rights himself in defensive attitude. There are lines in the libretto which, heard only once, remain in the mind forever as final definitions of certain experiences of love and grief. Some of these are sung by the henchman, Æthelwold. He is the eternal "man's man" who has occupied himself with battles in defense of his king's interest and never found time for love. Then, in Ælfrida he finds the inescapable woman. Though she is intended for the king as his bride her presence at his side brings Æthelwold himself to an extremity of need. He cries out:

> Ah, thy sweet look,
> Thine arrowy, sweet, sweet look!
> 'Tis sunk to the feather in my heart.

At the end of the opera he kills himself in desperate shame over his treachery. King Eadgar sings the obituary of the hero and his words bring something quite startlingly new to a theme as old as written literature: the intrinsic value of the human spirit at its best.

> Not all of us here,
> Nor all of England weeping,
> Should weep his worth,
> That was so young and blithe and bold,
> Whom the thorn of a rose hath slain.

> Wherefore let us hoard our tears for
>   a little sorrow,
> And weep not Æthelwold at all.

The plays, made to order under special circumstances, constitute only part of the burden that Edna Millay put dutifully upon her gift. There were crises of social life which gave gross affront to the most fundamental of her convictions and she could not withhold her protests. These took poetic form but — as she later knew to her chagrin — she was able at such times only to rear up the framework of a poem, gaunt and horrifying. To the lines with which she clothed the structure she could communicate her impotent rage but not the essence of compassion which she wished to memorialize.

There was, for example, her involvement in the Sacco and Vanzetti case. This *cause célèbre* enlisted the minds and the passions of many liberals who were convinced that a cruel miscarriage of justice threatened traditional liberties. Two political rebels, accused of armed robbery and murder, were tried and re-tried in the courts of Massachusetts but always, as their defenders insisted, under the shadow of hatred for their theoretical beliefs. Not men but their ideology was actually on trial and — again in the opinion of the protestants — revenge was the unmasked motive in which American society, through some of its officers, was permitting itself to indulge. Edna Millay was a participant in mass meetings held to call public attention to the crisis. She was eloquent also in a personal interview with the governor of Massachusetts and in a letter urging him to "exert the clemency which your high office affords."

When Sacco and Vanzetti were finally ordered to be executed, Edna Millay wrote the poem "Justice Denied in Massachusetts," a desperate and bitter threnody.

> Let us abandon then our gardens and go home
> And sit in the sitting-room.
> Shall the larkspur blossom or the corn grow
> under this cloud?
> Sour to the fruitful seed
> Is the cold earth under this cloud,
> Fostering quack and weed, we have marched
> upon but cannot conquer;
> We have bent the blades of our hoes against
> the stalks of them.

The unwilling, half-stifled protest that a reader makes in his turn against these utterances springs from the impression that a just and honest sentiment is being overdramatized. Is the abject surrender to despair really congenial to the poet's spirit or does this lamentation have to be brought under the charge of being tainted by hysteria? The conviction is clearly genuine but the excess of passion with which it is expressed still seems dubious. The literary

39

crisis is not ameliorated when the poet yields her mind to the most cliché of imaginings: "We shall die in darkness, and be buried in the rain."

It is right for a poet to be a participant in the affairs of everyday living. With her special talent for doing precisely this, Edna Millay could not withhold her word. Nor is it relevant that the guilt or innocence of the two men whose part she took is still a moot question. The respect must be paid her of considering anything she wrote as a work of art. Viewed in that light it becomes evident that poems written for occasions come forth misshapen at their birth by the influence of propaganda. In work that was truly her own even her bitterest protests against the will to destroy were informed by a still abiding faith; such poems reveal her militant spirit at its most staunch. The weakness of "Justice Denied in Massachusetts" must be attributed to the fact that it was not nourished by an inner will but fed on the inadequate substitute of propaganda.

The most conspicuous of the poems that Edna Millay regretted having written is *The Murder of Lidice*. The occasion that prompted it was one of such monstrous horror that any excess of passion in response to its tragedy must be condoned in advance. The leveling of a Czechoslovakian town and the mass martyrdom of all its men, women, and children — Hitler's revenge for the killing of one of his most sinister lieutenants — offers a theme for lamentation too big to be encompassed in words. Edna Millay might have reminded herself that it is well to save one's tears for a little sorrow. Lidice could, indeed, not be wept at all.

Judgment against its quality as literature may be left to her. As she once wrote: "It has some good lines, but not many, and not very good. This piece should be allowed to die along with the war which provoked it. I only hope its death will not be so lingering as that of the war itself."

It must be added that the occasions which, as she would have said, pressed in on her did, in the end, evoke true poetic expression. The theme of war recurs again and again in the later poems. The sonnets are full of references to its shadow on the earth. Each of these, matured by contemplation and refined by discipline, is moving; each informs the mood with the pathos of remembering all the opportunities that, in his heedlessness and haste, the "shining animal, man," has managed to throw away. She has only to speak again in her own voice to have all of her eloquence and her freedom from pretense restored. In the last of the sonnets the questions so long debated between mind and heart are resolved at last into a compassionate grief which can be endured even if heart and mind — and Edna Millay, too — still do "not approve," still are "not resigned."

The longest distraction from her personal preoccupations which Edna Millay was led into came from the temptation to experiment with translation. All her life she read Latin poetry for nourishment to mind and to technical facility; for her own pleasure she frequently translated poems from French and Spanish into English. A protracted period of effort in this field began when George Dillon suggested that she examine, in the form of a preface to a proposed volume, his translations of Baudelaire's *Les Fleurs du Mal*. In preparing to do so she was trapped inadvertently, as she has reported, into translating first a single line of one poem, then the whole poem, and finally many more. In the end George Dillon received her gratefully as fellow translator and, in their book, the initials of each identifies the maker of the contribution.

As translator Edna Millay was conscientious and sympathetic. She felt the much-misrepresented spirit of Baudelaire to have been "tortured and idealistic." His impulse was "to conquer ugliness by making beauty of it." She wished neither to purify him of what have been regarded as his perversities nor to tamper with his technique in the use of verse forms. She hoped to "scratch the iron palate of the modern reader" and gave him a stout, stimulating taste of the true Baudelaire. What must be made clear is that the mind of the poet was given its special turn by an ironic distaste for hypocrisy. What he defiantly calls his "flowers of evil" are, in truth, nothing so obviously poisonous and malign. They are really — as Edna Millay says in her preface, unable to resist the temptation to turn criticism into poetry — "flowers of doubt . . . flowers of grief . . . flowers forced on the sterile bough of the mind's unblossomy decay."

She was determined to clothe Baudelaire's verse forms in English leaving the original anatomy intact. Accordingly she edged her way patiently toward "the unbridgeable gulf between two minds" and at last found a rapport. She studied the psychological differences between two cultures in their predilection for one meter over another. She acquainted herself with disparities between two languages in resources of vocabulary. She took account of unlikenesses of emphasis resulting from such matters as the greater intensity of vowels in French. Her treatments of the poems of Baudelaire reproduce his forms as nearly as is possible. But they achieve much more than that. One feels that ideas and passion, conveyed by Edna Millay, could have originated in no other intelligence than that of Baudelaire.

Though her approach was as respectful — totally respectful — as only that of a fellow artist can be, she found herself renewed, as poet, by association with a compatible spirit. (She, too, was tortured and idealistic.) Inevitably she brought something of her own into these re-creations. Baudelaire's garden of the flowers of evil blooms under a foreign sky; it regains life in a new soil. The climate of Edna Millay's intelligence tends to heighten the color of images and to develop in them greater detail of design. What is formal in Baudelaire's language — stylized and formulary — is set aside sometimes in favor of effects more casual and — in English, certainly — more evocative of receivable emotion. In the poem called "Les Sept Vieillards" a literal translation of one line would be "These seven hideous monsters had the air of being eternal." Edna Millay renders it, putting the reference to monsters into an earlier line: "Somehow I knew they were eternal,— I could tell."

In her preface to the book of poems, presented in both French and English, Edna Millay speaks of her treatments as "adaptations" rather than as translations. They may be included in the small body of literature which, in effect, makes new land to fill in the unbridgeable between two minds. This is what Robert Lowell has done brilliantly in what he prefers to call his "imitations" of the poems of many other poets. Without doing violence to original intent — even when literal translation seems to be impossible — these two artists of adaptation manage to absorb the influence of one man's spirit, extend that influence across time, and draw it into sympathetic association with the values of an essentially different culture.

Edna St. Vincent Millay has been praised extravagantly as the greatest woman poet since Sappho. She has also been dismissed with lofty forbearance as a renegade from the contemporary movement in poetry and sometimes been treated almost as a traitor because she never broke defiantly with the past. But both eulogy and denigration seem to hang upon her figure like whimsical investitures. Neither costume suits the occasion when her enduring presence rises up before us to bespeak a mind that has not lost its vigor. Her talent shrugs off these irrelevances — still staunch, still self-reliant, and still self-fulfilled. What we hear is a voice urging

43

upon us the will to survive, uttering its sentiments with the grace and gravity of an intense and highly personal awareness. The fervor has not been dissipated from her words nor has the lucidity faded from her patterning of them into idea and conviction. In its most ardent moments the performance shows the same familiar spontaneity, disciplined into elegance without loss of power. It should be enough to call this talent unique among those that have appeared in our time. Rejecting comparison and eluding classification, an artist who has spoken so clearly and so persuasively seems tacitly to remind us that there is really no acute need to try to grade achievement according to an established formula or to consider austerely, precisely, what place may be accorded to her in the hierarchy of genius.

But acceptance of this gift as a natural phenomenon need not preclude the effort to discover its significance as a manifestation of the creative impulse in America. That she was peculiarly a product of our native way of life critics and the general public alike recognized when she first appeared. In the nymph of Greenwich Village phase she appeared to be the very embodiment of a characteristic and widespread spirit, roused by the circumstances of the time. As she grew older her temper was affected by other circumstances just as the temper of the country and the century was affected by new crises and new obligations. The tragic quality of the human experience became, for Edna St. Vincent Millay, ever more and more evident. It should not be suggested that the miseries of war, of depression, and again of war chastened her, mellowed her, or performed any of the improving operations which disaster is often said to perform on the docile. Her fundamental outlook did not change; she would seem to have been born with her special insights clear before her eyes. But her temperament was enriched and her intelligence was spurred to an ever more alert display of will by the pressure of many threats. Without any loss of wit, the early frivolity dropped away leaving her nature fully revealed as champion, even at a moment when calamities multiplied, of faith in "the shining animal's" ability to be reborn.

So, in the end, she was more surely the embodiment of the American outlook than she had been in the beginning. Indeed she enclosed the ethos of these United States in the twentieth century within the variety of her temperament. Even the contradictions and unresolved conflicts that tormented her were the same ones that have confused our culture. The granite of New England was in her and so was the flexibility of bohemia. She was American in her recklessness and in her reserves; in her mixture of audacity and decorous formality; in her devotion to learning and in her determination to put it to creative use; in her impulse toward rebellion, corrected and controlled by her respect for tradition; in her will to carry the battle to the enemy even when she knew the adversary to be the invincible one, death. The blend in her intelligence of traits derived from many sources of American vitality conveys the striking impression that she contained within herself important aspects of our native genius, alerted to a fine intensity of insight.

It is this absorbing — and, surely, durable — interest that claims for her a permanent place in the history of American poetry. She belongs to an impressive company of artists who came to maturity and found their voices during the second quarter of this century. Many of these have undertaken to explore the darkest caves of the secret mind of man and they have developed new poetic forms in which to record their experiences. Among them the figure of Edna St. Vincent Millay is conspicuous because she stands alone and in a blaze of light. It is impossible not to understand what she has to say, impossible not to be moved by the simple, direct, eloquent statements of her convictions. The world, which she had held no closer at the beginning of her life than she did at the end, gave her as much of pain as it did pleasure. Love, beauty, and life itself had all to be endured as well as enjoyed. But the human experience had meaning for her. The round of the seasons still kept to its pledge of rebirth and renewal. From that faith she drew the strength to impart dignity and beauty — as she said of Baudelaire's achievement — to even the most cruel phases of the adventure of our time.

⤳ Selected Bibliography

Works of Edna St. Vincent Millay

POETRY

Renascence and Other Poems. New York: Harper, 1917.
A Few Figs from Thistles. New York: Harper, 1920.
Second April. New York: Harper, 1921.
The Harp-Weaver and Other Poems. New York: Harper, 1923.
The Buck in the Snow. New York: Harper, 1928.
Poems Selected for Young People. New York: Harper, 1929.
Fatal Interview. New York: Harper, 1931.
Wine from These Grapes. New York: Harper, 1934.
Huntsman, What Quarry? New York: Harper, 1939.
Make Bright the Arrows. New York. Harper, 1940.
Invocation to the Muses. New York: Harper, 1941.
Collected Sonnets. New York: Harper, 1941.
Collected Lyrics. New York: Harper, 1943.
Poem and Prayer for an Invading Army. New York: Harper, 1944.
Mine the Harvest. New York: Harper, 1954.
Collected Poems. New York: Harper, 1956.

PLAYS

Aria da Capo. New York: Harper, 1920.
The Lamp and the Bell. New York: Harper, 1921.
Two Slatterns and a King. New York: Harper, 1921.
The King's Henchman. New York: Harper, 1927.
The Princess Marries the Page. New York: Harper, 1932.
Conversation at Midnight. New York: Harper, 1937.
The Murder of Lidice. New York: Harper, 1942.

TRANSLATIONS

Flowers of Evil, from *Les Fleurs du Mal* by Charles Baudelaire. New York: Harper, 1936. (With George Dillon.)

PROSE

Distressing Dialogues. New York: Harper, 1924. (Under pseudonym Nancy Boyd.)

47

JAMES GRAY

Letters of Edna St. Vincent Millay, edited by Allan Ross Macdougall. New York: Harper, 1952.

CURRENT AMERICAN REPRINTS

Collected Lyrics. New York: Washington Square Press. $.60.
Collected Sonnets. New York: Washington Square Press. $.60.
Letters of Edna St. Vincent Millay. New York: Universal Library (Grosset and Dunlap). $1.65.

Bibliography

Yost, Karl. *A Bibliography of the Works of Edna St. Vincent Millay.* New York: Harper, 1937. (See this volume for a listing of critical and biographical studies through 1936.)

Critical and Biographical Studies

Bogan, Louise. *Achievement in American Poetry, 1900–1950.* Chicago: Henry Regnery, 1951.

Davidson, Edward. "Edna St. Vincent Millay," *English Journal*, 16:671–82 (1927).

Gregory, Horace, and Marya Zaturenska. *A History of American Poetry, 1900–1940.* New York: Harcourt, Brace, 1946.

Humphries, Rolfe. "Edna St. Vincent Millay, 1892–1950," *Nation*, 171:704 (December 30, 1950).

Ransom, John Crowe. "The Poet as Woman," *The World's Body.* New York: Scribner's, 1938.

Sheean, Vincent. *The Indigo Bunting.* New York: Harper, 1951.

Taggard, Genevieve. "A Woman's Anatomy of Love," *New York Herald-Tribune Books*, April 19, 1931, p. 3.

Tate, Allen. "Miss Millay's Sonnets," *New Republic*, 66:335–36 (May 6, 1931).

Van Doren, Carl. *Three Worlds.* New York: Harper, 1936.

Wilson, Edmund. "Epilogue, 1952: Edna St. Vincent Millay," in *The Shores of Light.* New York: Farrar, Straus, and Young, 1952.

48